Badger Key Stages
History Starters

Book Two

Phil Suggitt

Badger Publishing Limited
26 Wedgwood Way, Pin Green Industrial Estate, Stevenage, Hertfordshire SG1 4QF
Telephone: 01438 356907 Fax: 01438 747015.

Cover photograph: Portrait of Henry VIII by Hans Holbein the Younger (1497/8-1543),
© The Bridgeman Art Library.

Introduction

What is a Starter?

The first phase of a lesson is 'prime time' for learning. To paraphrase the KS3 Strategy Training Materials for the Foundation Subjects, starters are about purposeful interactive whole class teaching. They aim to get the lesson off to a flying start. Starters are active, engaging and thought provoking.

What makes a really good starter activity? (A personal view.)

The most effective History starters are brief, lasting around five minutes.

I often find that some activities that I originally intended as starters take a great deal longer than I planned, and are actually more effective as main lesson activities. Many other teachers have had similar experiences.

In other subjects with a more generous KS3 time allocation, it may be possible to devote 10 minutes or more to the starter, but not in many History lessons.

A starter should not be over ambitious.

Sophisticated concepts or complex new input cannot be dealt with in 5 minutes. A starter has to be challenging, but not pitched so far beyond the pupils' comfort zone as to be impossible. On the other hand, the activity should not be too easy or trivial. Many of the starters in this book use pictures. This is not because visual material is 'easier' than text, but because it can be accessed more quickly.

A starter should not be predictable and repetitious.

Teachers need a wide repertoire of varied starters. A narrow range of activities that cater for a limited number of learning styles will not inspire pupils.

A starter should be fun, but not a 'game.'

A starter is a learning experience, not a form of light entertainment. Most of the 'games' in our society have winners and losers, elimination and a fierce competitive element. Although I am often told that boys thrive on such competition, the starters in this book try to avoid winners and losers, prizes and rewards. I cannot think of a worse start to a lesson than 'losing' a game, being eliminated early, or knowing that certain pupils are always going to be the likely winners. A good starter provides the opportunity for everyone to be a winner.

A starter should include everyone in the class.

There must be no passive 'spectators!'

A starter should link to the last lesson or the main part of the current lesson.

It should not be a 'bolt-on'. On average, the KS3 provision for History is 60-70 minutes per week. A starter that had no connection to the main part of the lesson would not only be wasteful, it would confuse the pupils.

Most starter activities are also good plenary activities.

Many of the best starters are designed by individual teachers for their own classes. A collection of 'off the shelf' starters cannot take account of the individual and personal needs of a particular class.

So why this book of starters?

At KS3, History is unlikely to be taught for more than one or two lessons, averaging 60-70 minutes per week. Many teachers would love to prepare a wide range of starters, but lack the time.

Secondly, many departments are small and cannot profit from the 'everyone design and share' approach.

Thirdly, starters can become predictable. Few would disagree with the principle of an engaging and inclusive start to a lesson, but no-one wants to hear pupils say 'Oh, this is the third time we have done this kind of starter… today.' A compendium of good starters can add to teachers' repertoire.

There is not always enough time to design, prepare and print starter materials for every lesson. It is hoped that the materials in this book will save time and inspire adaptations using different content.

Not all starters require a bank of resources to engage pupils. Many great starters are simple and take almost no preparation. A list of such 'low maintenance starters' has been included on page 5. These can be used in a variety of contexts.

Most History teachers adapt the broad NC outlines to their own situation, so there is a considerable national variation between the content and style of History lessons at KS3. The starters in this book have taken the most common and popular topics into account, but can easily be adapted to other content with a minimum of work.

Contents

No.	Title	Type
1	Life in c.1500	Change & Continuity
2	Society in 1500	Ranking
3	What did they wear?	Matchmakers
4	The English Reformation	Place that picture
5	Power and responsibility	Key words
6	Henry VIII	Contemporary portraits
7	Portraits	Me and them
8	Should Queen Elizabeth get married?	Choices
9	Paupers and vagabonds	Language of vagabonds
10	The Gunpowder Plot	Inferences from visual
11	What should Charles have done?	Quiz
12	Illustrations from witchcraft pamphlets	Visual stimulus
13	The Civil War	What's the question?
14	Why was Charles executed?	Interpreting quotes
15	The execution of Charles I	Comparing pictures
16	Should there be a Restoration?	Who said it?
17	The Levellers	Prediction
18	The Great Fire of London	Pictograms
19	The making of the UK	Stereotypes
20	The Industrial Revolution	Translation
21	What is an industrial revolution?	Key words
22	The Agricultural Revolution	Similarity & difference
23	Effects of the Railway Revolution	Actions & results
24	The British Empire in 1900	Map list
25	The Agricultural Revolution	Visual stimulus
26	Why was slavery abolished in the British Empire?	Ranking
27	19th century attitudes to women	Visual stimulus
28	Factory conditions	Classification
29	Attitudes to native peoples in the British Empire	Highlighting
30	People and their achievements	'Name and Fame' revision

24 low maintenance starters requiring little or no preparation

Recap

1	List 3 things you learnt last lesson.
2	What was the most important learning point from last lesson.
3	Summarise what you know in 5 bullet points.
4	Summarise what you know in 5 words.
5	Draw a timeline of events covered so far.
6	Draw a graphic summary of knowledge so far – mind map, flowchart, picture, etc.
7	In small groups, rehearse a mime of an event studied last lesson. Act it out to the rest of the class.
8	Talk for one minute about a topic covered.
9	Make up some 'odd one outs' about a topic covered.
10	Teach a partner the key point of last lesson.
11	Do a Chinese whisper with the key point of last lesson.
12	Make a list of questions to ask the teacher about last lesson or topic.
13	Make up some multiple-choice questions to ask the rest of the group.
14	Make up a subject related charade and perform it to the class.
15	Describe HOW you learnt last lesson, not WHAT you learnt.

Key Words

1	Teacher says key words, pupils write definitions.
2	Teacher says definitions, pupils write key words.
3	Spelling test on key words.
4	Invent a mnemonic to help people remember a key word.
5	The magic ruler – a pupil is given the magic ruler and thinks of a key word, term or person. They hand the ruler to someone else, who has to say something valid about the word, and then think of a new word. Repeat.

New Topic

1	Brainstorm all you know about a new topic.
2	List things you want to know about a new topic.
3	Set a homework where pupils have to find out something about the new topic to share at the beginning of the next lesson.
4	Draw a diagram or mind map to show your understanding of the topic before new learning.

Life in c.1500

Objective:

To identify aspects of life that have changed or remained constant over the period 1066-1500, 1500-1750.

Teaching point:

This is a flexible starter in which the initial pupil activity can be completed quite quickly, but the whole class discussion can be an open-ended activity. The length of the discussion may depend on the interest of the pupils. Pupils tend to make very few links with previous KS3 work, particularly if it was done in the last academic year. By comparing with 1066 pupils are encouraged to relate to previous work. Getting things 'right' is not as important as seeing that the pace of change was very slow in many aspects of medieval life. The 1750 column allows the pupils to extrapolate. Their responses can be used formatively, to see what they know or remember about, for example, the Reformation. Some teachers might want to omit this column, feeling that it is too difficult for particular classes, or may result in unhistorical guesswork.

What you will need:

Copies of Copymaster 1a for each pupil, Copymaster 1b Teachers' copy, copies of Copymasters 1c-e cut out into a set of cards, OR 1a as an OHT.

Time: 5-10 minutes

Key words: similarity, difference, continuity, change

Activity:

Issue Copymaster 1a and one large card from Copymasters 1c-e to each pair of pupils. Tell the class that the second column of 1a lists some true statements about Britain in c.1500, at the beginning of the Tudor period. This term they will be studying aspects of British history between 1500 and 1750. Remind the pupils that they studied Medieval Times, from 1066 onwards, in Year 7. Ask the pupils to tick the boxes in the L column if they think this aspect of life was much the same in 1066.

Ask the pupils to tick the boxes in the R column if they think this aspect of life will remain substantially unchanged in 1750.

Allow 5 minutes.

Either: Ask each pair to come to the front and write on the OHT their ideas about 1066 and 1750. Or draw a grid on the board, with the three dates. Pairs bring their three cards to the board and decide whether to put a card in all 3 columns. This approach appeals to kinaesthetic learners, but requires more resources and will take a lot longer. Or delete the L or R column, only have 2 columns.

Use answers as the basis for class discussion.

Challenge: To explain why some things might have changed or stayed the same since 1750.

Links to plenary: N/A

Life in c.1500

Much the same in 1066	LIFE IN 1500	Much the same in 1750
	Most people were poor – they just about grew enough to feed themselves.	
	Most people lived in the countryside, in small villages.	
	Most people worked on the land.	
	There were many more sheep than people.	
	There were huge forests.	
	There were many wild animals in the forests, like boars and pigs.	
	The biggest industry was cloth making.	
	There was no UK; England, Scotland and Wales were separate.	
	Most people went to church every week.	
	England was a Roman Catholic country. The Pope was head of the church.	
	London was the only large town – the rest were just big villages.	
	Most people didn't travel far from their village.	
	Only rich children were educated, the rest were put to work.	
	The king or queen was the person with the most power. They ruled with the help of the richest people.	
	England wasn't a very rich or important European country.	
	Men had more power than women and did most of the important jobs.	

Life in c.1500

Much the same in 1066	LIFE IN 1500	Much the same in 1750
Yes	Most people were poor ~ they just about grew enough to feed themselves.	No
Yes	Most people lived in the countryside, in small villages.	Yes
Yes	Most people worked on the land.	Yes
Yes	There were many more sheep than people.	No
Yes	There were huge forests.	No
Yes	There were many wild animals in the forests, like boars and pigs.	No
No	The biggest industry was cloth making.	Yes
Yes	There was no UK; England, Scotland and Wales were separate.	No
Yes	Most people went to church every week.	Yes
Yes	England was a Roman Catholic country. The Pope was head of the church.	No
Yes	London was the only large town ~ the rest were just big villages.	No
Yes	Most people didn't travel far from their village.	Yes
Yes	Only rich children were educated, the rest were put to work.	Yes
Yes	The king or queen was the person with the most power. They ruled with the help of the richest people.	No
No	England wasn't a very rich or important European country.	No
Yes	Men had more power than women and did most of the important jobs.	Yes

Life in c.1500

Most people were poor ~ they just about grew enough to feed themselves.

Most people lived in the countryside, in small villages.

Most people worked on the land.

There were many more sheep than people.

There were huge forests.

There were many wild animals in the forests, like boars and pigs.

Life in c.1500

The biggest industry was cloth making.

There was no UK; England, Scotland and Wales were separate.

Most people went to church every week.

England was a Roman Catholic country. The Pope was head of the church.

London was the only large town ~ the rest were just big villages.

Most people didn't travel far from their village.

Only rich children were educated, the rest were put to work.

The king or queen was the person with the most power. They ruled with the help of the richest people.

England wasn't a very rich or important European country.

Men had more power than women and did most of the important jobs.

Society in 1500

Objective:

To put the main social groups of early Tudor England into a ranked order. To decide on the criteria for ranking.

What you will need:

Copymaster 2 as an OHT, or as copies for each pupil or pair, as preferred. Or as sets of 4 cards.

Teaching point:

Some pupils will automatically assume that you want them to put the groups into a hierarchy of wealth and social importance. Others will ask you what kind of order you want them to be grouped in. It is up to the pupils to decide on the criteria. Some pupils put labourers and citizens first, as they did most of the work, others put all groups above the gentlemen, who they regard as privileged.

Key words: hierarchy, the words on Copymaster 2

Activity:

Explain that in 1500 people saw each other as belonging to distinct social groups. Without further comment, ask the class to rank the social groups in order.

a. Very kinaesthetic version. Groups of four are given the cards, and stand in line. Some classes like the movement, teamwork and have to read the cards to each other and collaborate. This version is likely to take longer than b or c.

b. Less kinaesthetic version. Pairs or individuals are given the information as cards and asked to rank them, working at a desk.

c. Speedy version. The information is given on an OHT transparency. Pupils rank the groups on a mini-whiteboard or paper.

Discuss ~ ask pupils to justify their findings.

Challenge: Pupils could be asked why the social groups do not explicitly mention women. When I tried this activity one girl made a fifth card from scrap paper. She wrote 'women' on the card and placed it at the top of her list. She said 'They didn't really value women.' She had a point.

Links to plenary: This activity is a good 'lead in' to activities about rigid class boundaries.

YEOMEN

They did not own farms.
They rented them from gentlemen or citizens.
They grew food, and sold the food they did not eat at the market.
Most were quite well off.

LABOURERS

They were mostly farm workers.
They worked for yeomen or the gentry.
They did not earn very much, and were sometimes called 'the labouring poor.'
They lived in rented cottages.

THE NOBLES

A small number of people with titles such as dukes and earls. They were very rich and owned lots of land. They lived in very grand houses. They helped the king rule England.

GENTLEMEN

Most of the GENTRY owned land. They were well off. They owned good houses. They did all the important local jobs like being Justices of the Peace, who organised law and order.

CITIZENS

A small number of people who lived in towns.
Some were quite poor, others were well off.
They were merchants or craftsmen.

What did they wear?

Objective:

To identify costumes from different centuries.

Teaching point:

To fully enter into an investigation of a historical period, pupils need to know what typical people looked like. Pupils enjoy 'pairing up' the couples. This starter has value for formative assessment. Pupil answers will tell you if the class has any concept of changes in dress. From 1500 to 1700 there were small changes in the clothes of working people but, to emphasise this point, the Copymaster drawings are exactly the same. Point out that the vast majority of people never wore 'fashions'. Many pupils think all people dressed like royalty and the aristocracy!

What you will need:

Class copies of Copymasters 3a-c cut out in a set, put into an envelope. OHT copies of Copymasters 3a-c.

Key words: There are many technical words to describe the intricacies of costume and fashion. They are not necessary for this activity.

Activity:

Tell the class that the pictures represent typical costume for rich and ordinary people in c.1500, c.1600 and c.1700. There are six couples.

Match the couples from each period, and put them in chronological order.

The task needs quite a lot of room, making it an ideal pair activity.

Alternative: as above, but only issue the six fashionable figures. Issue the six ordinary pictures and repeat the activity as a plenary, or as the starter for the next lesson.

Challenge: Ask the class to account for the lack of dramatic change in the costume of ordinary people.

Links to plenary: See alternative activity, above. This starter is suitable for lessons on any aspect of everyday social life.

What did they wear?

Rich and ordinary ~ 1520's

What did they wear?

Rich and ordinary ~ 1620's

Rich and ordinary ~ 1720's

The English Reformation

Objective:

To classify items as belonging in a Roman Catholic or Anglican church at the time of the Reformation.

Teaching point:

This activity was first tried with a third, Puritan church. There were too many items for some pupils to handle. It would be possible to repeat this activity when studying Puritanism, comparing a Puritan and Anglican church.

What you will need:

Copymasters 4a-b, with the pictures cut out in a set for each pair. Copies of Copymaster 4c, one for each pair, blown up to A3.

Key words: Reformation, the words on Copymasters 4a-b

Activity:

This activity was inspired by the party game 'Stick the tail on the donkey!' It is intended as a recap of the main differences between the Catholic and Protestant church at the time of the English Reformation, and should follow a lesson on this topic.

Either:

Pairs are given a set of the small pictures from Copymasters 4a-b, and a copy of 4c.
Tell the class to put the items in the correct church.

Or:

Enlarge the pictures, put a little blu-tak on the back. Issue one per pair. Divide the board into Catholic and Anglican halves. Pupils fix their pictures on the correct side of the board. The other pupil in the pair has to explain the choice.

This is a more active kinaesthetic activity that involves less materials and preparation.

Challenge: Which of the changes do you think would have been the most dramatic for ordinary people? Why?

Links to plenary: N/A

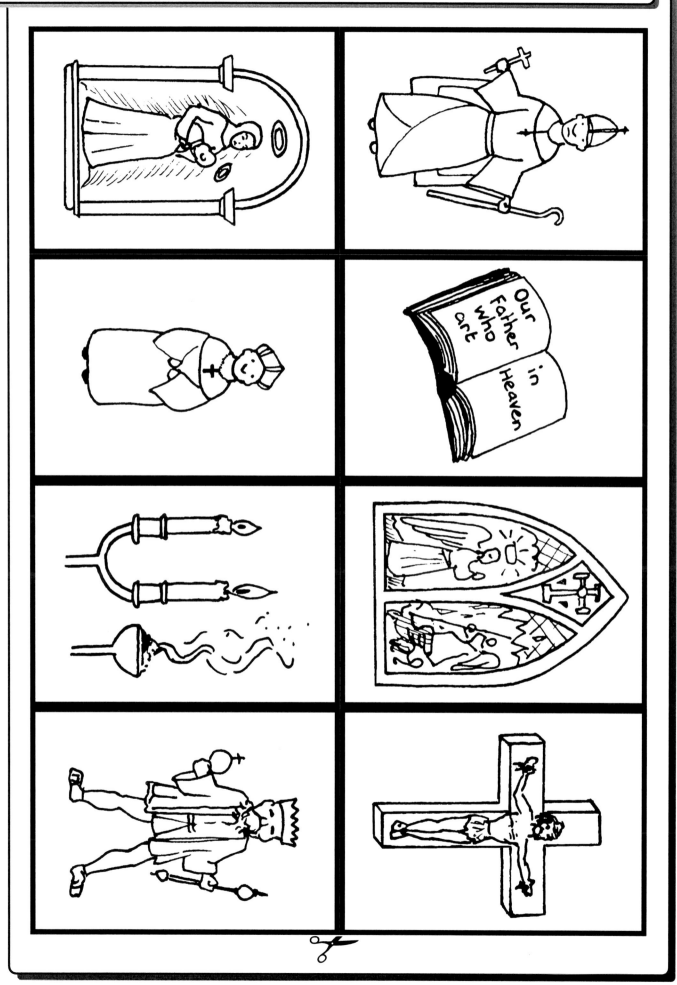

The English Reformation

	Roman Catholic
	Protestant-Anglican

Power and responsibility

Objective:

To select the correct definition for key words relating to the lesson and unit.

Teaching point:

The key words were selected for introductory lessons about power and society in c.1500. Words can be added or subtracted to suit the needs of the class or the lesson. Pupils may be familiar with some of the words due to their previous work. This key word approach can be repeated with different words at the beginning of every new topic. The large cards can be laminated and saved for repeated use.

Originally this activity involved a series of cards for the definitions and key words. Individual pupils had to connect a definition with a key word held up and read out by the previous pupil. This is very effective with small groups, but with large groups it leaves many pupils as uninvolved spectators. Pupils can write the words next to the definitions and save Copymaster 5a in their books or files.

Key words: All the words on the cards!

What you will need:

Copies of Copymaster 5a, definitions, for each pupil or pair. One larger teacher copy each of Copymasters 5a/b, cut into cards. If possible, print the two teacher sets of cards, key words and definitions, on different coloured paper for easier identification. Blu-tak.

Activity:

If possible, put the pupil sheets on the desks before the lesson, or give them out as the class enter. Say that there are some key words that everyone needs to understand when investigating certain historical questions.

Explain that the page contains a series of definitions. You will hold up a key word and they have to highlight or underline the appropriate definition on the sheet.

Ask for answers. Ask a pupil to come to the front, pick the correct definition from the larger teacher cards at the front, and fix the word and definition on or around the board. (If the cards are mounted near the board they can remain as visible reminders for as long as necessary.)

Challenge: N/A

Links to plenary: In the Plenary, hide the definitions, hold up the key cards again and see how many the class can remember.

Power and responsibility ~ definitions

The king or queen who ruled the country.	The Houses of Lords and Commons together, who helped to make decisions about how the country was run.
How the country is run or the people who rule the country.	People with titles, who were usually rich and important.
The head of the Catholic church.	A part of Parliament. Members were chosen by the richer landowners.
A part of Parliament. The nobles and most important church leaders.	People who lived with or near the king ~ his family, servants and important noble friends.
False or distorted ideas intended to influence how people think.	Christians who believed the Pope was head of the church. The only church in England in 1500.
A small group of rich and important people chosen by the monarch to give 'private' advice about ruling the country.	

Power and responsibility ~ key words

Monarch	Parliament
Government	Nobles
Pope	House of Commons
House of Lords	Royal Court
Propaganda	(Roman) Catholics
Privy council	

Henry VIII

Objective:

To make deductions from a Tudor portrait.

Teaching point:

This popular portrait of Henry VIII has been selected because it can be interpreted without a great deal of historical knowledge. Many pupils are fascinated by the contemporary symbolism employed in many Renaissance paintings, but their sophistication renders them unsuitable for starter activities. It is intended that the main part of the lesson would involve a detailed study of more challenging contemporary paintings. Activities such as starter 7 could be useful introductory exercises in the study of propaganda and portraits. However, the activity can be done without previous work on portraits.

What you will need:

Copies of Copymaster 6a for pupils, Copymaster 6b ~ possible pupil responses.

Key words: portrait, propaganda, impression

Activity:

Issue Copymaster 6a. If possible, enlarge the page to A3 so that the pupils have more room to annotate the portrait.

Ask the pupils to arrow and label aspects of the portrait that give a positive impression of the king, that 'make Henry look good'.

Typical responses are shown on Copymaster 6b.

Discuss responses. The discussion could lead into the main part of the lesson, with information on Holbein and the use of royal propaganda. (Holbein was Henry's favourite court painter and was commissioned to paint several images of the king. Many copies of the finished painting were made, to be displayed around the country and sent abroad.)

I would like to thank Marilyn Kelly of Cheshunt School, Herts, for the ideas for this starter!

Challenge: Ask pupils a more open question such as 'What impression of Henry VIII does the artist give?' Label the features that give this impression.

Links to plenary: Tell the class that the painting was made after 1537. Henry was at least 47 and in a bad state of health. Does this alter their perceptions of the portrait?

Portrait of Henry VIII by Hans Holbein the Younger (1497/8-1543), © The Bridgeman Art Library.

Pupil sample responses

- Big broad shoulders ~ powerful

- Standing with legs apart ~ confident

- Richly decorated clothes imply wealth

- Lots of rich jewellery

- Muscular, strong legs

- Hand on hip implies confidence

- Dagger symbolises power

- Prominent codpiece suggests virility, masculinity

- Richly decorated carpet and wall hangings ~ luxury

- Shoes and impractical clothes show he doesn't have to do manual work

- Face suggests confidence, self-satisfaction

Portraits

Objective:

To empathise with a Tudor monarch's motives for being painted.

Teaching point:

This task could support work on QCA unit 7, Images of an Age. This approach asks the pupils to move from 'How would *you* feel?' to 'How would *people from the past* have felt?' in a simple attempt to move from the personal to the historical, from everyday empathy to historical empathy. A starter cannot achieve a great deal on one isolated occasion, but this approach can be repeated ('little and often') in other historical contexts. For example, 'How would you feel if you were a soldier on the eve of battle?' then 'How do you think the soldiers felt on the eve of the battle of Marston Moor?' elicits a lot of similar responses, but also encourages some high order thinking, such as 'They would feel even worse because they were fighting their own people, maybe even relatives.' 'A lot of them were very religious. Maybe they weren't frightened because they really thought God would get them through.' 'Life was harder and crueller then. People would be more used to death.' 'There isn't one answer. There would be huge differences. Some people would be really worried and think about their families. Some would be really scared, others would be really up for it. People are different.'

What you will need:

Mini-whiteboards are useful but not essential. Sample responses provided on Copymaster 7.

Key words: portrait, image, impression

Activity:

Write the following question on the board: If you were having your portrait painted (or photographed) how would you want to look? (If the person sitting next to you was the painter, what instructions would you give them?)

Give an example, such as happy, good, neat hair, etc.

Give the pupils two minutes to write down some ideas, using mini-whiteboards or paper. Discuss the responses, but do not record them.

Then ask a second question: If you were a *Tudor monarch*, how would you want to look/present yourself in a painting?

Tell the class that this is a more difficult task. Some responses may be identical to the first task, but some will be different because of the differences in time and the motives for making the painting. Ask the class for an example, e.g. 'confident'.

Challenge: N/A

Links to plenary: The main body of the lesson would be concerned with Tudor portraits and propaganda.

Portraits

How would you like your portrait to look?

Some typical responses:

Make me look:

- good
- pretty
- handsome
- well dressed
- in fashionable clothes
- realistic
- smiling/happy
- my best
- get my best side
- flattering
- in my favourite clothes
- in my sports wear
- holding my pet
- as I really am

How do you think Tudor monarchs wanted to look?

- Powerful
- Strong
- Fair
- Honest
- Confident
- Handsome or pretty
- Attractive
- A winner
- All things to all men
- Rich
- Important
- Wise
- In charge
- Healthy
- Miss out any bad bits like having a big nose or huge ears

Should Queen Elizabeth get married?

Objective:

To consider how sensible and practical were the marital options open to Elizabeth I. To appreciate the political choices involved in Elizabeth's decision not to marry.

Teaching point:

Sometimes History can be all death, doom and disaster. Pupils (not just girls) enjoy studying happier topics such as Elizabeth's choice of men. It is only with hindsight that the decision to remain the Virgin Queen appears a sound one.

What you will need:

Copies of Copymaster 8 for each pair or individual.

Key words: marriage (often spelt wrongly!)

Activity:

Issue Copymaster 8.

Explain that Queen Elizabeth was 'by far away the best marriage to be had in Europe.' (Neale, J.E. [1934] Queen Elizabeth I, Jonathan Cape, London [Pelican reprint, 1973])

Pupils usually know that Elizabeth did not marry. Remind them that rulers did not usually marry for love, but for political reasons.

a.   Pupils put a ☺ or a ☹ next to each factor. (From Elizabeth's point of view.)

b.   For each balloon, pupils tick the factor which they think was the most influential in forming Elizabeth's choice.

Ask pupils to justify their choices. This starter can be a brief activity or the prelude to a discussion.

Challenge: N/A

Links to plenary: N/A

Should Queen Elizabeth get married?

I'm young, I'm very intelligent and I'm the most important woman in England. Everyone expects a queen to marry. All women marry. Who shall I marry?

A. Shall I marry AN ENGLISH NOBLEMAN? Lots of them want to marry me and some of them are very good looking. If I marry into one family, the other families will be jealous. He might want to tell me what to do.

B. Shall I marry KING PHILIP II OF SPAIN? He's head of one of the strongest and richest countries in Europe. He's a Roman Catholic ~ Spain is a Catholic country. He was married to my half-sister, Mary. He is unpopular in England after the loss of Calais.

C. Shall I marry a foreign prince (like Archduke CHARLES OF AUSTRIA)? Austria is a strong country. He is a Catholic. England will have to be involved in the regular wars and disputes between the countries of Europe.

D. Shall I marry NOBODY? No one thinks a woman is strong enough to rule alone. I won't upset the nobles by favouring one particular family. I won't have a child ~ an heir to the throne. Some people will think I am unnatural and strange.

Paupers and vagabonds

Objective:

To decipher and create sentences written in the language of Tudor vagabonds.

Teaching point:

This activity is a suitable starter for a lesson on poverty and crime in the Tudor period. Several textbooks contain longer lists of the slang language used by some Tudor vagabonds.

What you will need:

Copies of Copymaster 9a for the class, Copymaster 9b, best as an OHT, mini-whiteboards are useful but not essential.

Key words: rogue, vagabond

Activity:

Tell the class that the London underworld used a peculiar 'language of rogues' in Tudor times.

Issue Copymaster 9a. If possible, project 9b as an OHT.

Ask the pupils to 'translate' the sentences into modern English. Remind pupils not to call out their translations before others have finished.

Translations of the sentences on 9b:

'Some horse thieves gathered together to have a good drink at the White Horse Inn, in honour of their friend Robert who had been hung on the gallows that very morning.'

'William climbed into a gentleman's London house at midnight. He planned to rob him of his money, but he was discovered. A servant hit William on the head and he escaped by the skin of his teeth.'

Challenge: Ask pupils to write an original sentence in vagabonds' cant. Pupils could substitute modern and vagabond words when writing during the main part of the lesson.

Links to plenary: Pupils could write some of their original sentences on the board for the rest of the class to translate.

Paupers and vagabonds

Bread ~ pannum

Coat ~ togman

Corn ~ grannum

Drink ~ bouse

Eyes ~ glaziers

Gallows ~ chats

Good ~ bene

Hat ~ nab-cheat

Head ~ nab

Horse ~ prancer

Horse thieves ~ priggers of prancers

House ~ ken

London ~ Rome-vill

Nose ~ a smelling cheat

Pig ~ a grunting cheat

Rob ~ filch

Teeth ~ crashing cheats

Tongue ~ a prattling cheat

"Some priggers of prancers gathered together to have a bene bouse at the White Prancer Inn, in honour of their friend Robert who had swung from the chats that very morning."

"William climbed into a gent's ken in Rome-vill after twelve bells. He planned to filch his coin, but he was discovered. A servant hit William on the nab and he escaped by the skin of his crashing cheats."

The Gunpowder Plot

Objective:

To make inferences and tentative hypotheses from a visual clue, the signature of Guy Fawkes.

Teaching point:

This starter is effective as part of a first or second lesson on Anti-Catholicism and the Gunpowder Plot. It could also be used when teaching a lesson on crime and punishment.

What you will need:

Copymaster 10a as an OHT or pp slide. Alternative ~ Copymaster 10b.

Key words: torture, stress

Activity:

Display Copymaster 10a as an OHT or pp slide.

Explain that the top signature shows how Guy Fawkes usually signed his name. The second signature is from Guy Fawkes' confession, in which he admits he planned to blow up the Houses of Parliament.

Ask the pupils to work in pairs. For 2 minutes they discuss reasons why the two signatures are so different.

Responses could be written on a mini-whiteboard or rough paper.

Of all pupils who have tried this activity, 80% suggest Fawkes was bullied or tortured. Other common answers are that he was extremely frightened or exhausted.

A brief discussion leads pupils towards such questions as:

- who was he?
- what did he do?
- if he was tortured, was he really guilty?

Some classes might finish this task so quickly that an additional visual challenge could be provided, such as Copymaster 10b.

Challenge: Ask pupils to write 5 questions about Copymaster 10b, or what historical questions about the Plot 10b would help to answer and which questions it would not help to answer.

Links to plenary: N/A

Public Record Office, SP 14/216 nos. 54 and 101.

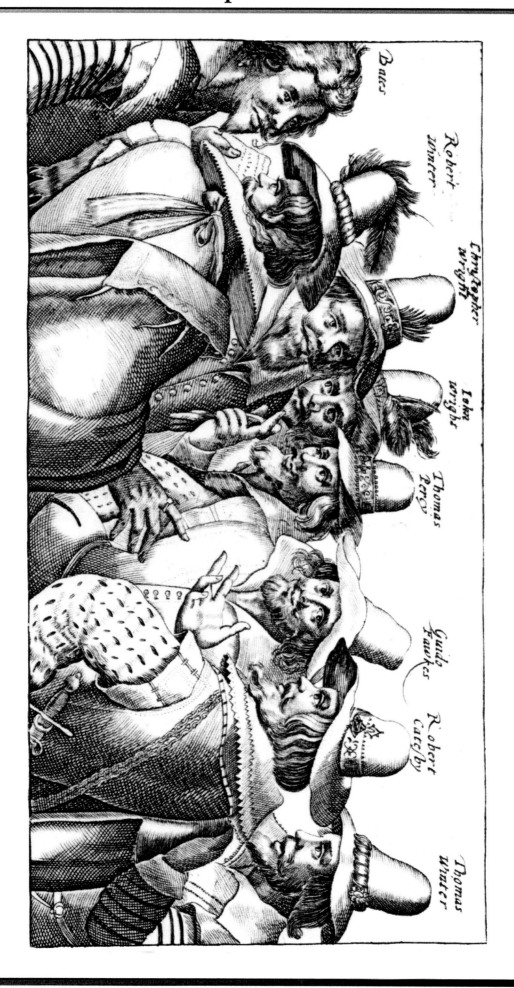

The Gunpowder Plot Conspirators, 1606 (engraving), German School (C17th), © The Bridgeman Art Library.

What should Charles have done?

Objective:

To consider Charles I's options when he had to make key decisions. To use hindsight and historical knowledge to select the best option.

Teaching point:

This is a useful starter for a lesson on the causes of the Civil War. It assumes that pupils have some prior knowledge of the religious and governmental problems of previous Tudor and Stuart monarchs. Pupils enjoy doing multiple choice magazine quizzes ~ this is a historical adaptation. Some pupils may get the impression that Charles was a fool. It is easy, with hindsight, to see how Charles' policies were ill-advised.

Key words: inevitable, hindsight

What you will need:

Copies of Copymaster 11a for each pair or individual member of the class, Copymaster 11b Teachers' answer sheet.

Activity:

Explain that a civil war between King and Parliament was not inevitable ~ it was not bound to happen. King Charles I was faced with many decisions that would affect his relations with his subjects.

Ask pupils to read Copymaster 11a and circle Charles' best options. This can be done by individuals or pairs. They do not have to guess what really happened, but use their knowledge of the period to decide what they think would have been the best option.

Challenge: Pupils underline the policy that they think Charles really followed.

Links to plenary: The main body of the lesson (or series of lessons) will be about the events leading up to the war. Pupils could be asked 'Which was Charles' worst error of judgement?'

What should Charles have done?

Who should Charles marry?

A noble European Protestant
A noble English Protestant
A noble European Catholic
No-one, like Elizabeth I

How should Charles deal with religion?

Continue to lead a moderate Anglican church
Make the Anglican church more Catholic
Make the Anglican church more Puritan

How should Charles raise the money he needed?

Invent new taxes and collect them without asking
Parliament, close Parliament down if it complains
Give Parliament some of the things they want
in return for giving him more money from taxes
Borrow money from European bankers

How should Charles deal with Puritan Scotland?

Do nothing ~ let the Scots carry on with their Puritan ways
Try to make the Scots' church like the English one
Allow the Scots to carry on with their
religion in return for taxes and support

Badger Key Stage 3 History Starters

What should Charles have done?

Who should Charles marry?

A noble European Protestant
A noble English Protestant = ✓
A noble European Catholic = C
No-one, like Elizabeth I

How should Charles deal with religion?

Continue to lead a moderate Anglican church = ✓
Make the Anglican church more Catholic = C
Make the Anglican church more Puritan

How should Charles raise the money he needed?

Invent new taxes and collect them without asking
Parliament, close Parliament down if it complains = C
Give Parliament some of the things they want in return for
giving him more money from taxes = ✓
Borrow money from European bankers

How should Charles deal with Puritan Scotland?

Do nothing ~ let the Scots carry on with their Puritan ways
Try to make the Scots' church like the English one = C
Allow the Scots to carry on with their religion in return for
taxes and support = ✓

Badger Key Stage 3 History Starters

Illustrations from witchcraft pamphlets

Objective:

To devise/generate questions from two picture source illustrations from witchcraft trial pamphlets.

What you will need:

Copies of Copymaster 12 for the class and as an OHT if possible, mini–whiteboards.

Teaching point:

The 'stimulating picture' is a highly effective starter, especially when used to introduce a new topic. In this case, contemporary woodcut illustrations are used to launch a lesson on witchcraft and superstition.

Key words: N/A

Activity:

Issue Copymaster 12, which can also be displayed as an OHT.

Alternative a. Ask pupils to write down five questions they want to ask about the pictures. This short activity can lead into a discussion on perceptions of witchcraft and witch stereotypes.

Alternative b. Ask pupils to write down up to five things the pictures suggest about witches in the 16th and 17th centuries. Possible responses include:

(They thought…)

- Witches were old women
- Witches were ugly
- Witches were threatening and mean
- Witches had small pets
- Some of the pets look like cats and dogs, others like small demons
- Some of the pets had names, or could speak
- The pets bit people
- The pets licked or kissed the witches
- Witches carried sticks, possibly due to old age
- Some witches knew each other
- They hung witches

Challenge: N/A

Links to plenary: N/A

The Wonderful Discoverie of the Witchcrafts of Margaret & Philip Flower 1619
© Copyright The Trustees of The British Museum

'The apprehension and confession of three notorious witches at
Chelmsforde...', London: Edward Allde, [1589]. Lambeth Palace Library.

The Civil War

Objective:

To recall factual information about the Civil War by suggesting possible questions for which the answer has been provided.

Teaching point:

'This is the answer, what is the question?' is a technique that can be applied to virtually any subject matter.

What you will need:

Copymaster 13a, as an OHT or a printed page for the class, Copymaster 13b possible questions, mini-whiteboards are useful but not essential.

Key words: The ones on the Copymaster.

Activity:

This is a good revision activity after the class has studied the events of the Civil War.

Explain that the information on the OHT (or printed Copymaster) consists of the answers to a series of questions about the English Civil War.

Pupils have to note down a possible question for each answer. Mini-whiteboards can be used for this. Point out that there could be more than one possible question.

Work through an example orally:

Answer: A civil war. Hopefully a pupil will provide a question such as 'What is the name given to a war between sides from the same country?'

For some pupils, this activity may be too challenging. The level of challenge can be reduced by issuing Copymaster 13b as cards, asking pairs of pupils to match them with the answers.

Challenge: Most of the answers on Copymaster 13a are closed and factual. It is much more difficult to devise questions when the answers are more involved, conceptual explanations. This exercise can encourage very high level thinking. If this approach is used, the number of questions needs to be reduced, or it becomes a main activity rather than a starter.

Links to plenary: Ask pupils to devise their own answer/question. Other pupils can work out the question as part of the plenary.

The Civil War

Cavaliers
Marston Moor, Naseby and Edgehill
Carisbrooke Castle
January 1649
The New Model Army
Oliver Cromwell & Thomas Fairfax
Because many had short hair
London, the S and E of England
Soldiers who wanted a more equal, democratic society after the war

The Civil War

Possible answers

What nickname was given to the Kings' side?
What were the three main battles of the war?
Where was Charles imprisoned at the end of the second war?
When was Charles' trial and execution?
What was the name of the Parliamentary army trained by Cromwell?
Name two Roundhead generals.
Why were the Parliamentary troops nicknamed 'roundheads'?
In which parts of the country did Parliament have its strongest support?
Who were the Levellers?

Why was Charles executed?

Objective:

To offer brief interpretations of a contemporary quotation.

Teaching point:

A starter activity cannot do justice to a sophisticated question such as 'Why was Charles I sentenced to death?' There are, in fact, times when a starter can trivialise a situation. This starter aims to introduce one of the main issues involved by the use of a 'key quote'. Asking pupils to interpret a brief contemporary comment can be a very effective starter type, as long as the source is not so obscure and difficult that pupils find it completely baffling.

What you will need:

Copies of Copymaster 14 as an OHT or paper copies, mini-whiteboards are useful but not essential.

Key words: execute, execution, treason, traitor

Activity:

Show Copymaster 14 as an OHT or paper copies.

Ask the pupils what they think the Earl's comment has to do with the decision to execute Charles.

Pupils jot down an idea, which can be discussed as the introduction to a lesson on the contemporary debate about how Charles should be dealt with.

Possible interpretations of Manchesters' comment:

'We' = Charles' enemies, the Parliamentary side.

Charles believed in the Divine Right of Kings. To oppose the king was an act of treason that would be punishable by death. If the Parliamentarians lost they would be executed as traitors.

The Earl realises that Charles would always be a danger as long as he lived, because he would always try to attract support and regain his power if he was exiled, imprisoned or forced to work as a constitutional monarch with limited powers.

Challenge: N/A

Links to plenary: N/A

It matters not to the king how often he fights. We have to be more careful. If we fight him a hundred times and yet only lose once he will still be king and we will be hanged.

The Earl of Manchester, a Parliamentary leader, 1644

The execution of Charles I

Objective:

To identify similarities and differences between two versions of the execution of Charles I in 1649.

Teaching point:

This activity can be used before or after pupils have studied the trial and execution of Charles I. Other comparisons of accounts of the execution focus on contradictory accounts or pictures which are based on the other source to be compared. The two versions selected are superficially similar. There is no firm evidence that either artist was an eye witness. A was produced by a Dutch artist. The historian John Bowle states that B 'is less inaccurate than the melodramatic versions more widely known, and its starkness evokes the grim and wintry occasion.'
(J.Bowle, *Charles the first* [1975], London: Weidenfeld & Nicholson, p.115)

What you will need:

Copies of Copymasters 15a-b for the class, OHTs of Copymasters 15a-b. Copymaster 15c lists some similarities and differences.

Key words: execution, scaffold, contemporary

Activity:

If possible, distribute Copymasters 15 a-b before or as pupils enter the room.

Say that the two illustrations are contemporary, they were made near to the time of the events they portray. The artists and exact dates are unknown.

This is a good pair activity, as the pictures take up a lot of room if each pupil is working with two images.

Ask the pupils to divide the mini-whiteboard or piece of paper into two. Write down as many significant similarities and differences as you can see.

Discuss pupils' ideas.

Challenge: Is one version a more reliable account of what really happened than the other?

Links to plenary: During the lesson, the class can be introduced to other pictorial and oral accounts of the execution. During the plenary they could be asked to list five facts they are certain of.

The execution of Charles I

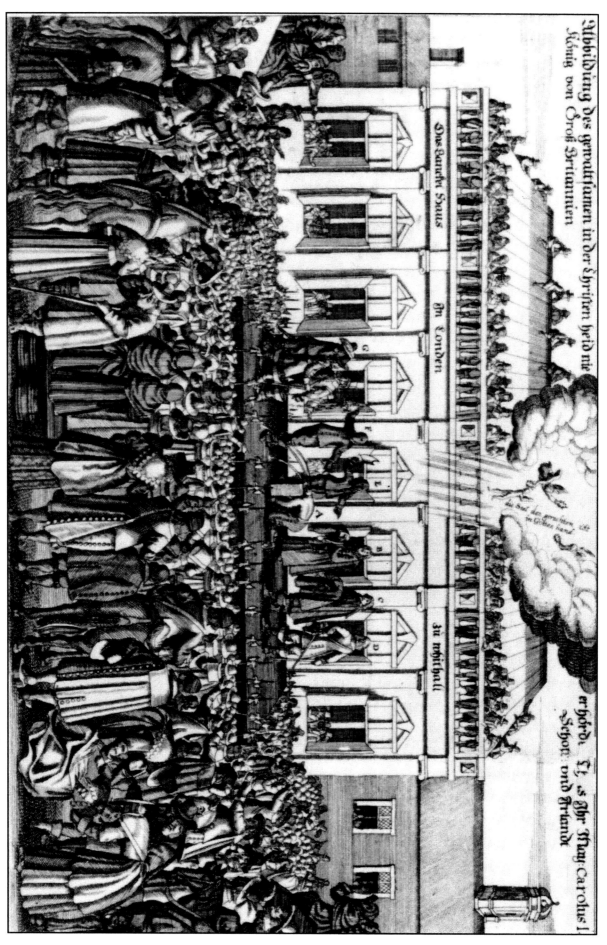

The beheading of King Charles I (1600-49) 1649 (engraving), Dutch School (C17th), © The Bridgeman Art Library.

The execution of Charles I

Execution of Charles I (1600-49) at Whitehall, January 30th, 1649 (engraving), English School (C17th), © The Bridgeman Art Library

The execution of Charles I

Similarities

- Large crowd
- People on the roofs of buildings
- Wooden block, axe
- Raised scaffold
- Soldiers around the scaffold
- The execution is taking place in front of a large building with tall windows, surrounded by other stone buildings

Differences

- Executioner is masked in A
- Much larger crowd in A
- In A some of the crowd are in open windows behind the scaffold, and on the roof tiles themselves
- A shows Heaven ~ angels etc
- A labels some of the buildings
- More soldiers on the scaffold in B
- More soldiers around the scaffold in B
- The crowds in B are all male and all wear hats
- There is a barrier around the scaffold in B
- A shows events after B ~ the king has been beheaded and his head is raised to the crowd

Should there be a Restoration?

Objective:

To match contemporary views with contemporary groups or individuals.

What you will need:

Copies of
Copymaster 16.

Teaching point:

Matching contemporary views to contemporary statements can be an effective way of testing pupils' understanding of the attitudes held by the groups they have studied. It is important that pupils move beyond 'stereotypical empathy'. At the very least, point out that not all individuals in a group would necessarily share similar opinions. In this case, the pupils are asked to draw on their knowledge of the Civil War and Interregnum to predict likely attitudes to the Restoration.

Key words: Restoration

Activity:

Tell the class that a group of MPs were thinking of restoring the monarchy by inviting the son of Charles I to return from Europe to be crowned as Charles II.

Issue Copymaster 16.

Ask pupils to read the statements in the word balloons and link them with the 'talking heads' on the page.

This could be done by drawing lines and arrows.

More kinaesthetic ~ cut out the balloons and place them above the right person.

Answers

How can we trust the son of Charles I? He will want revenge on everyone who fought against his father! 2

Let's have a king back. He will restore all the fun things that the Puritans have banned! 1

Bringing back a king to work with Parliament is our last chance. None of our experiments in governing the country have worked. 3

If we have a king again, things might get back to normal. We don't want everything to be turned upside down all the time, we just want to get on with the harvest. 4

We don't need a king of any kind. Our problems would be solved if everyone had a vote! 5

Challenge: N/A

Links to plenary: Ask pupils to think of a reason why a person might NOT hold the opinion typical of the group they linked them with at the start of the lesson.

Should there be a Restoration?

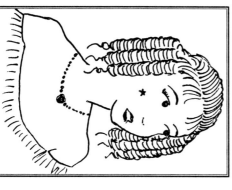

1 An actress

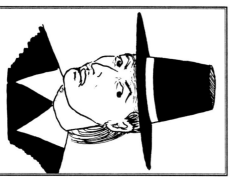

2 Someone who signed Charles I's death warrant

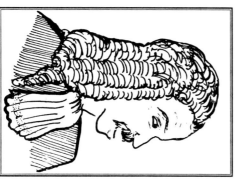

3 A leading MP

4 A farming family

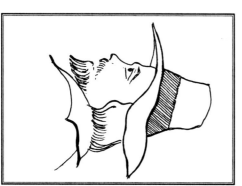

5 An ex-soldier who used to be a Leveller

How can we trust the son of Charles I? He will want revenge on everyone who caused the death of his father!

Let's have a king back. He will restore all the fun things that the Puritans have banned!

Bringing back a king to work with Parliament is our last chance. None of our experiments in governing the country have worked.

If we have a king again, things might get back to normal. We don't want everything to be turned upside down all the time, we just want to get on with the harvest.

We don't need a king of any kind. Our problems would be solved if everyone had a vote!

The Levellers

Objective:

To decide which of the Leveller demands are true today.

Teaching point:

This activity is a useful formative assessment task in that it highlights what pupils know about our modern political system. It is hard for pupils to appreciate the emergence of radical political and social ideas in the 1640s and 1650s if they lack a basic understanding of modern democracy! In previous years, I found that I took such a basic understanding for granted when in fact many pupils were very unsure of many details. The introduction of Citizenship will be a great help. The list of Leveller demands, originally printed in the pamphlet '*The Agreement Of The People*,' has been adapted into modern English.

What you will need:

Copymaster 17a as an OHT and/or pupil copies. Copymaster 17b Teacher's page.

Key words: Leveller, radical

Activity:

Tell the class that after the end of the first Civil War in 1647 there was a lot of discussion about the way the country should be ruled. The Levellers were a group who put forward some ideas. There was strong support for the Levellers' ideas in the victorious New Model Army.

(Teachers who prefer starters which do not involve any explanation could set the scene at the end of the preceding lesson. A homework could be set: 'Having won the war, what should Parliament do with the king? How should England be ruled?')

Pupils read the list of Leveller demands and underline the ones that have become reality.

Challenge: To understand why the Levellers made these particular demands. To explain why many people in the 17th century strongly opposed some of the Levellers' demands. This question can be developed in the main body of the lesson. It is too sophisticated to be dealt with as a starter.

Links to plenary: This starter would lead to a main activity on radical ideas. The plenary would relate to the main activity.

The Levellers

1. The country should be ruled by a parliament.

2. Each parliament should be elected every two years.

3. Each part of the country should be fairly represented in parliament.

4. Everyone over 21 should vote, not just the richer people. (Women and servants should not vote because they might be easily influenced by their masters.)

5. Laws should be fair and equal for all people.

6. Law courts should work more cheaply so that everyone can afford justice.

7. All laws should be made by an elected parliament, not a king.

8. All the different kinds of Puritans should be allowed to worship freely.

From *The Agreement of the People*, 1647, a pamphlet produced by the Levellers.

The Levellers

Demands which eventually became law are underlined.

1. <u>The country should be ruled by a parliament.</u>

2. Each parliament should be elected every two years. *Not practical. Parliaments would change before they had time to see through their ideas. We have adopted the idea of regular parliaments and regular elections, however.*

3. <u>Each part of the country should be fairly represented in parliament.</u>

4. Everyone over 21 should vote, not just the richer people. (Women and servants should not vote because they might be easily influenced by their masters.) *We have adopted the principal of equality. Everyone over 18 can vote. Women received an equal vote in 1928. Today hardly anyone works as a servant, but they can vote!*

5. <u>Laws should be fair and equal for all people.</u> *Most pupils agree, but some argue that our laws aim for equality in principle, but in practise favour certain sectors of society.*

6. <u>Law courts should work more cheaply so that everyone can afford justice.</u> *Some pupils agree that this has been achieved. Others point out that money can buy the best lawyers.*

7. <u>All laws should be made by an elected parliament, not a king.</u> *Today the monarch signs acts of parliament, but plays no part in their creation.*

8. All the different kinds of Puritans should be allowed to worship freely. *Today all religions are tolerated, not just forms of Protestant Christianity.*

From *The Agreement of the People*, 1647, a pamphlet produced by the Levellers.

The Great Fire of London

Objective:

To translate information from a pictorial to a visual medium, by interpreting simple pictograms that represent facts about the Great Fire of London.

What you will need:

Copies of Copymaster 18 for each pupil.

Teaching point:

This task can be used to revise material covered in the previous lesson. Alternatively, it can be used at the very beginning of a study of the fire, to quickly give the class access to a lot of basic information. Pictograms are often used as a reading aid for very young children, but they can be a very useful way of giving information in an active way, so that the pupils can then use the information in more challenging, higher-level activities.

Key words: N/A

Activity:

Issue Copymaster 18. Asks pupils to write down the meaning of the pictograms in the spaces provided. (To save paper, answers could be written on a mini-whiteboard or paper.)

Challenge: Ask pupils to design their own pictogram sentence to convey another fact they know about the Great Fire.

Links to plenary: (See challenge, above.) Some pupils could draw the pictograms they have designed on the board. The rest of the class interpret them.

The FIRE of London, 1666.

1. The summer of 1666 was ☼ with

   little  .

2. London was full of 🏠 .

3. The fire started in a 🥖 shop.

4. Farmers sold 🐎 so people could escape

   with their goods.

5. People fought the fire with 🪣 and 💦 .

6. The 💨 E spread the fire.

7. To stop the fire 💥 BOOM!

8. 13,000 🏠 and 88 ⛪ were burnt down,

   ▨ of the City of London. 6 people ⚰ .

The making of the UK

Objective:

To write English stereotypes of Scots, Welsh and Irish people.
To consider the historical origins of prejudice.

What you will need:

Copymaster 19c,
ideally as an OHT,
mini-whiteboards are
useful but not essential.
Copymasters 19a-b as
OHTs/cards if desired.

Teaching point:

This starter is intended for the beginning of a lesson or series of
lessons on the union of England, Scotland, Wales and Ireland /
United Kingdom. Dealing with prejudices and stereotypes can be
a delicate issue. This starter tackles the issue directly. With some
classes, a more cautious approach is necessary. It involves very
little preparation. This type of starter is very brief, but it is vital
that a class discussion follows. (Type of starter that moves directly
to the next phase of the lesson.)

Key words: stereotype, prejudice, xenophobia

Activity:

Remind the class of the meaning of the words 'stereotype' and 'prejudice' (and 'xenophobia' can
also be introduced). If these terms have not been used previously, they could be prominently
displayed on cards (Copymaster 19a).

Ask the pupils to list English stereotypes of a Scots, Welsh and Irish person.

Pupils can work alone or in pairs. For speed, list rather than write in full sentences.

Use mini-whiteboards for this activity, if available.

Compare pupil ideas. Typical responses are given on Copymaster 19b, which could be used if
desired.

Show (preferably with OHP) the stereotypical picture, Copymaster 19c.

Challenge: Ask pupils to think of reasons for the historical origins of such stereotypes.
Typical responses are given on Copymaster 19b, which could be used if desired. Then
link to the main activities ~ relations between the four nations, and the gradual creation
of the UK.

Links to plenary: As a plenary, pupils could be asked to name an aspect of the
stereotype that is a distortion of the past historical situation (such as the poverty in
Ireland, the Jacobite rebellions, etc).

Stereotype

Ways in which people or things can be similar, or typical.

Prejudice

To 'pre-judge' someone or something. To form an opinion without enough evidence.

Xenophobia

Hatred or distrust of foreigners.

The making of the UK

Typical pupil responses

Stereotypes ~ Ireland

- Primitive
- Poor
- Aggressive
- Big drinkers
- Navvy
- Thick, or at best uneducated ~ Irish jokes
- Catholic
- Patriotic
- Also ~ accent/terrorist

Stereotypes ~ Scotland

- Usually focus on dress; sporran, tartans, kilt
- Bagpipes
- Big drinkers ~ whiskey
- Mean with money ~ Scottish jokes
- Wild, warlike Highlanders ~ Hadrian's wall to keep them out
- Accent
- Very patriotic, historic rivalry with England
- Keen on soccer but not currently very successful

Stereotypes ~ Wales

Many pupils find this difficult. This can be related to the peaceful and successful integration of Wales and England in Tudor times. Popular negative images of the Welsh did not develop.

Stereotypes focus on recent times, such as:

- Coal miners
- Keen rugby players
- Sheep farmers

Possible reasons

- Ignorance
- Lack of understanding of other ways of life.
- Communications. Until recently few people travelled very far and had little idea about people who lived in other parts of the UK.
- The stereotypes support the idea that the Scots, Welsh and Irish were inferior.
- Exaggerations of former conditions ~ e.g. Ireland used to be poor, few people were educated.
- Fear and suspicion of 'foreigners'.

PUNCH, OR THE LONDON CHARIVARI.—SEPTEMBER 30, 1865.

ERIN'S LITTLE DIFFICULTY.

BRITANNIA. "YES, MY DEAR! THAT'S THE SORT OF DRILLING TO DO *HIM* MOST GOOD!"

Badger Key Stage 3 History Starters

The Industrial Revolution

Objective:

To translate statistical information into a literary form.

Teaching point:

This starter is suitable for an introductory lesson on the Industrial Revolution. Pupils need a big but accessible picture of the Industrial Revolution before they can deal with finer detail. Translating information from one form to another is generally accepted to be one of the best ways to understand information. After the class has completed the starter, it may be useful to briefly discuss the value of translating information.

What you will need:

Copies of Copymasters 20a-b, and/or an OHT, mini-whiteboards are useful but not essential.

Key words: It is presumed that 'industry' and 'revolution' will already have been discussed.

Activity:

Issue Copymasters 20a-b.

Ask the pupils to write a very short paragraph explaining what the statistics mean. Discuss pupil responses.

After the class has completed the starter, it may be useful to briefly discuss the value of translating information.

Challenge: By outcome ~ the responses can be very simple or sophisticated.

Links to plenary: The main part of the lesson should give a more detailed outline of the main changes in the first phase of the Industrial Revolution. Pupils could redraft their original paragraphs in the light of their improved understanding.

The Industrial Revolution

1. Population

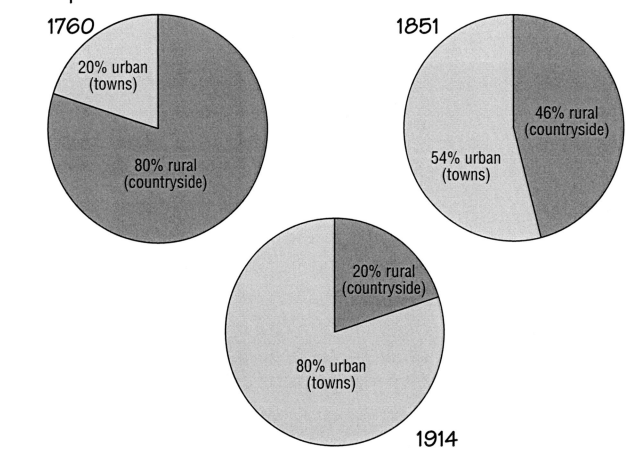

Population in millions

Year	Population
1751	10.70m
1801	15.90m
1851	27.40m
1914	41.50m

2. Population distribution

1760
- 20% urban (towns)
- 80% rural (countryside)

1851
- 54% urban (towns)
- 46% rural (countryside)

1914
- 80% urban (towns)
- 20% rural (countryside)

The Industrial Revolution

3. Percentage of national income

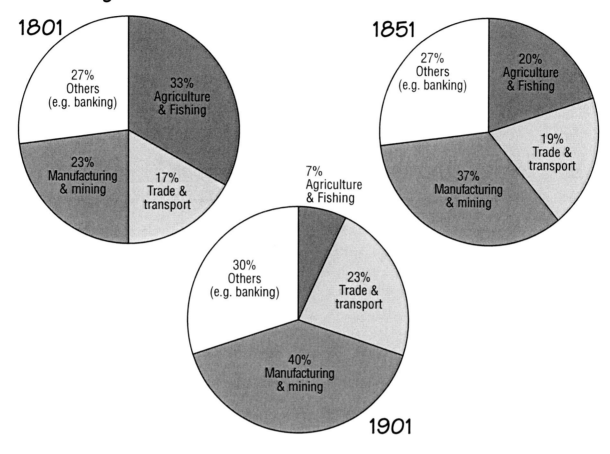

1801
- 27% Others (e.g. banking)
- 33% Agriculture & Fishing
- 23% Manufacturing & mining
- 17% Trade & transport

1851
- 27% Others (e.g. banking)
- 20% Agriculture & Fishing
- 19% Trade & transport
- 37% Manufacturing & mining

1901
- 7% Agriculture & Fishing
- 30% Others (e.g. banking)
- 23% Trade & transport
- 40% Manufacturing & mining

4. Industrial production

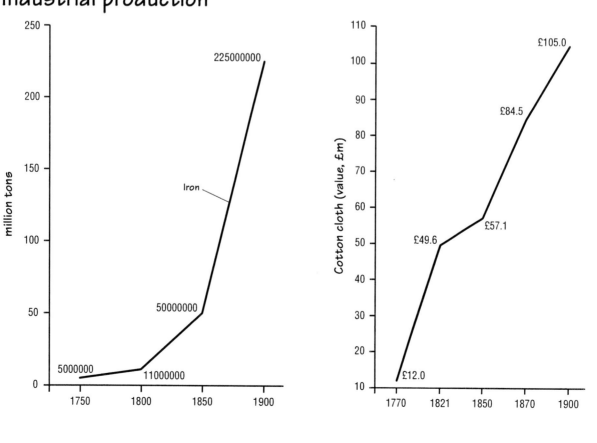

Left graph — million tons (years 1750–1900):
- 5000000
- 11000000
- 50000000
- 225000000
- Iron

Right graph — Cotton cloth (value, £m) (years 1770–1900):
- £12.0
- £49.6
- £57.1
- £84.5
- £105.0

What is an industrial revolution?

Objective:

To consider misconceptions about the word 'revolution'.

Teaching point:

All pupils know the word 'revolution', but hear it used in different contexts. This starter is useful in a lesson dealing with an outline 'big picture' of the first Industrial Revolution.

What you will need:

Copies of Copymaster 21.

Key words: revolution

Activity:

Issue Copymaster 21. Explain that it contains some different ways in which the word is used and confused.

In each case, pairs have to give another word or phrase for revolution. Answers can be written on the sheet, on paper or on mini-whiteboards.

Typical answers:

    a. Horrible

    b. Turned around, spun

    c. New and different

    d. (Instant) Change in government

    e. A huge/dramatic gradual change

    f. A huge change

Discuss pupil ideas before moving on to a study of the main aspects of the Industrial Revolution.

Challenge: Ask the pupils which two sentences use the word in a similar way.
   (e and f are both about dramatic technological changes.)

Links to plenary: N/A

a. There was a revolting smell in Joe's room.

b. The Big Wheel revolved 10 times.

c. At the fashion show the models wore some revolutionary new designs.

d. In 1917 there was a revolution in Russia. The people overthrew the government and changed the way the country was run.

e. From c.1760 to c.1850 Britain had the worlds' first Industrial Revolution.

f. In the last few years there has been a revolution in the world of computers.

The Agricultural Revolution

Objective:

To compare plans of a village before and after enclosure, identifying the main changes.

What you will need:

Copies of Copymaster 22a and 22b for the class, mini-whiteboards useful but not essential.

Teaching point:

The village before and after enclosure joins the Roman legionary as one of the subjects most commonly drawn in History lessons! This approach uses the diagram at the beginning of the lesson, rather than as the main activity. Whilst it may have been appropriate for pupils taking a GCSE Social and Economic course to meticulously draw and label such diagrams, KS3 pupils have far less time available. Their time is better spent in thinking about the implications of the agricultural changes. This activity encourages pupils to deduce a lot of information that has traditionally been given to them. This starter is useful as an introduction to a lesson on the Agricultural Revolution. It is expected that the class already have a simple 'big picture' of the first Industrial Revolution.

Key words: enclosure, agriculture, fallow

Activity:

Tell the class that there were some dramatic changes in the way the land was farmed during the late 18th and early 19th centuries.

Issue Copymasters 22a and 22b. Read the titles on the two pictures.

Pairs of pupils study the two pictures, and record the significant changes.

A discussion of the pupils' responses can lead into the main part of the lesson, concerning the causes and effects of enclosure.

Typical pupil responses

- The three large fields have been replaced by many smaller, rectangular fields.
- The narrow strips of land have gone.
- Hedges and fences separate the land.
- All the land is being farmed ~ the fallow field has gone.
- The common land has gone ~ animals are kept on individual farms.
- There are more individual farms.

Challenge: What can be deduced from the diagrams about the reasons for the changes? What questions arise from the diagrams?

Links to plenary: N/A

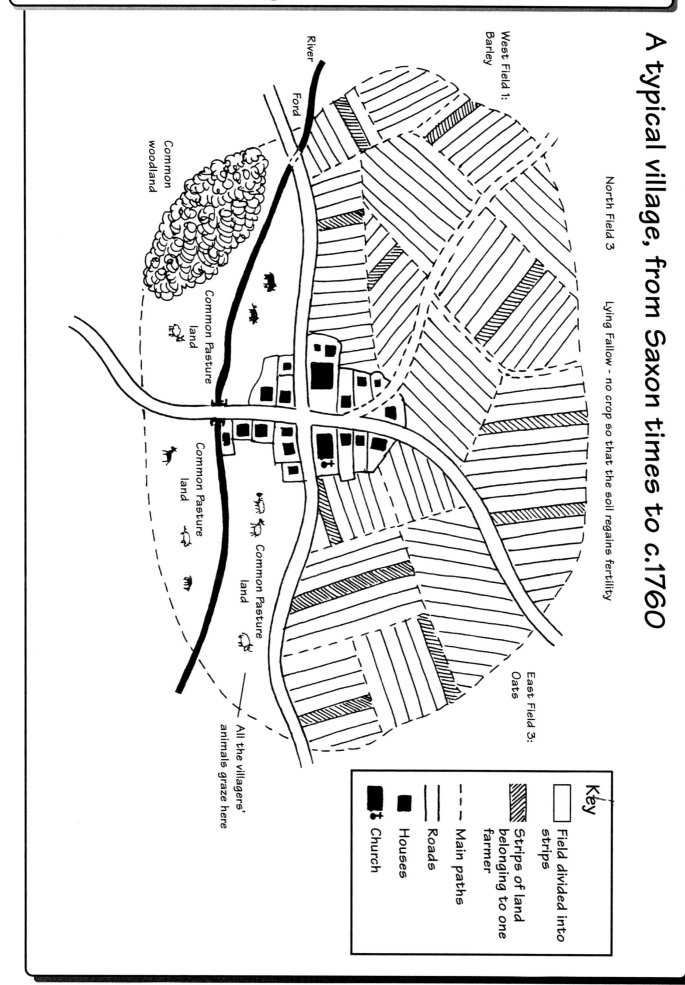

A typical village, from Saxon times to c.1760

River

Ford

West Field 1:
Barley

North Field 3

Lying Fallow - no crop so that the soil regains fertility

East Field 3:
Oats

Common woodland

Common Pasture land

Common Pasture land

Common Pasture land

All the villagers' animals graze here

Key

Field divided into strips

Strips of land belonging to one farmer

Main paths

Roads

Houses

Church

The Agricultural Revolution

The same village in c.1820, after enclosure

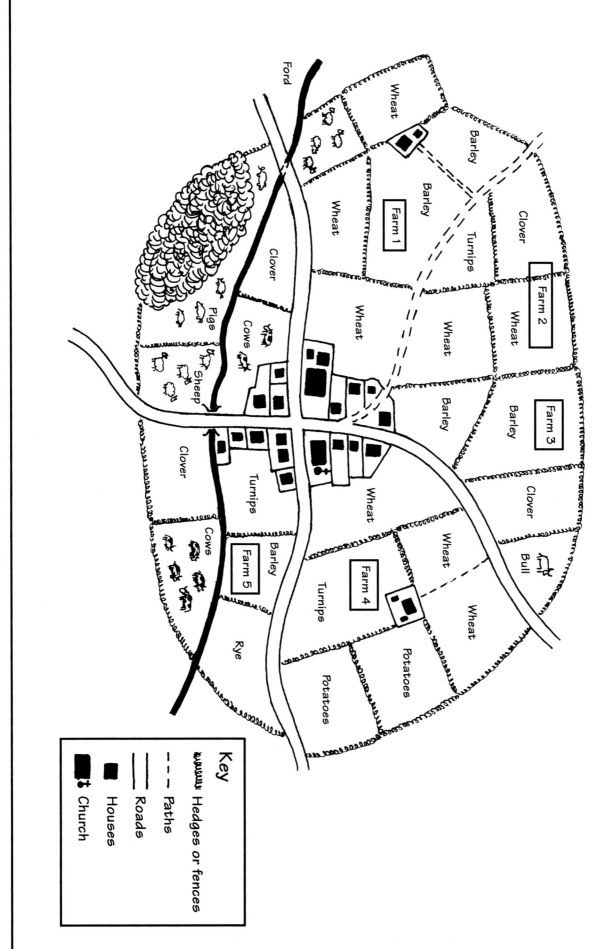

Key

- ⌇⌇⌇ Hedges or fences
- ----- Paths
- ——— Roads
- ■ Houses
- ☖ Church

Effects of the Railway Revolution

Objective:

To explain the reasons for some of the changes made by the Railway Boom of the 1840s.

Teaching point:

This is an adaptable starter that can be used as a low-challenge matching exercise, or as a higher challenge 'explain the statement' task. This activity can work well with classes that are about to study the effects of railways as well as classes that have just completed their study.

What you will need:

Copymasters 23a-b cut out in a set for each pair. (See alternatives listed under 'activities', below.)

Key words: N/A

Activity:

Cut out Copymasters 23a-b into sets of cards for each pair. Print each one on a separate colour. Ask pupils to match each result with the most appropriate explanation.

Twelve results are provided on the Copymaster, too many to deal with in five minutes. You can select the number your class can cope with. Alternatively, five cards could be introduced at the beginning of the lesson, and five more in the plenary.

Challenge: Issue pairs of pupils with the results statements only. Pupil A takes the top card and reads it to pupil B. B has to explain the statement. B then reads the next card to A, and roles are reversed. The pairs deal with as many cards as they can in five minutes.

Links to plenary: Copymaster 23a is not a complete list. Pupils could write down another result for their partner to explain.

Effects of the Railway Revolution

RESULTS

a. Seaside towns developed (Blackpool, Southend, Brighton, etc).

b. National sports leagues began.

c. National daily newspapers.

d. Many shops carried more stock at cheaper prices.

e. Townspeople could eat fresh milk and fish.

f. Many Turnpike Trusts, Coach and Canal companies went out of business.

g. Richer people moved to suburbs away from town centres.

h. There was a high demand for coal, iron and steel.

i. Time became standardised.

j. Many Irish people moved to work in England.

k. There was a boom in the pottery industry.

l. A big increase in letter writing.

Effects of the Railway Revolution

EXPLANATION

Ordinary people could afford to go on seaside day trips.	Before railways, it cost too much and took too long to play distant away games.
Before railways, a paper printed on Monday would take several days to be distributed around the country.	Railways reduced the cost of transporting goods.
Fresh food could be delivered to shops before it went off.	Railways were faster, safer and cheaper than other forms of transport.
Wealthier people could move out of the dirty town centres and 'commute' from pleasant suburbs.	Coal was used for fuel. Iron and steel was used for the engines, carriages and the track.
For timetables to work, trains had to arrive and depart at the times stated.	Thousands of Irish 'navvies' were needed to build the railway system by hand.
Delicate pottery and glassware could be transported for long distances with far less chance of breakage.	Cheap pre-paid stamps were put on letters, which were delivered by train.

The British Empire in 1900

Objective:

To list the places that were once part of the British Empire.

Teaching point:

One of the best ways to begin the study of an empire is to study a 'snapshot' of the empire at the height of its powers and at its largest extent. This approach works equally well with the Roman and British Empires. Seeing the extent and location of the empire helps pupils who are unsure of the concept. This activity can also tell you a lot about the prior knowledge and geographical understanding of your class.

What you will need:

Copies of Copymaster 24a or Copymaster 24b, Teacher copy 24c.

Key words: empire, commonwealth

Activity:

If possible, enlarge Copymaster 24a or b to A3 size, so that people can work on it together and write on the sheet.

Alternative a. Issue Copymaster 24a. Ask the pupils to make a list of countries that once were part of the British Empire. Pupils use paper, mini-whiteboards or write the names and numbers of the places they know around the map. Say that the names of some of the countries have changed since 1900. Encourage educated guesses. The Copymaster includes the first letter of each country, as a clue.

Alternative b. Issue Copymaster 24b and proceed as above. On Copymaster 24b the first letters have been removed so that the activity is more challenging.

Alternative c. Issue Copymaster 24b. For three minutes, pupils use the blank map on Copymaster 24b. Then show the map with the first letters of the countries, on Copymaster 24a, for a further two minutes. This can be shown using an OHP.

Discuss the list, which leads on to the main lesson question, 'How and why did Britain take over so many foreign lands?

Challenge: See activities, above.

Links to plenary: N/A

The British Empire in 1900

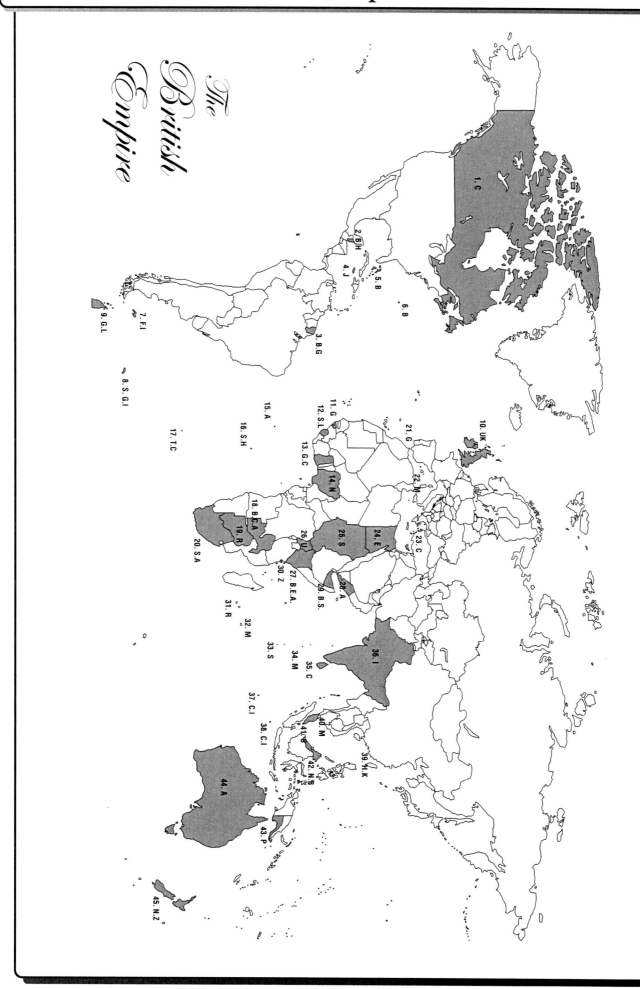

The British Empire

1. C
2. B.H
4. J
5. B
6. B
3. B.G
7. F.I
9. G.I
8. S. G.I
11. G
12. S.L
15. A
16. S.H
17. T.C
13. G.C
14. N
21. G
10. UK
22. M
18. B.C.A
19. R
20. S.A
26. U
25. S
24. E
23. C
27. B.E.A.
30. Z
29. B.S.
28. A
31. R
32. M
33. S
34. M
35. C
36. I
37. C.I
38. C.I
40. M
41. S
39. H.K
42. N.B
44. A
43. P
45. N.Z

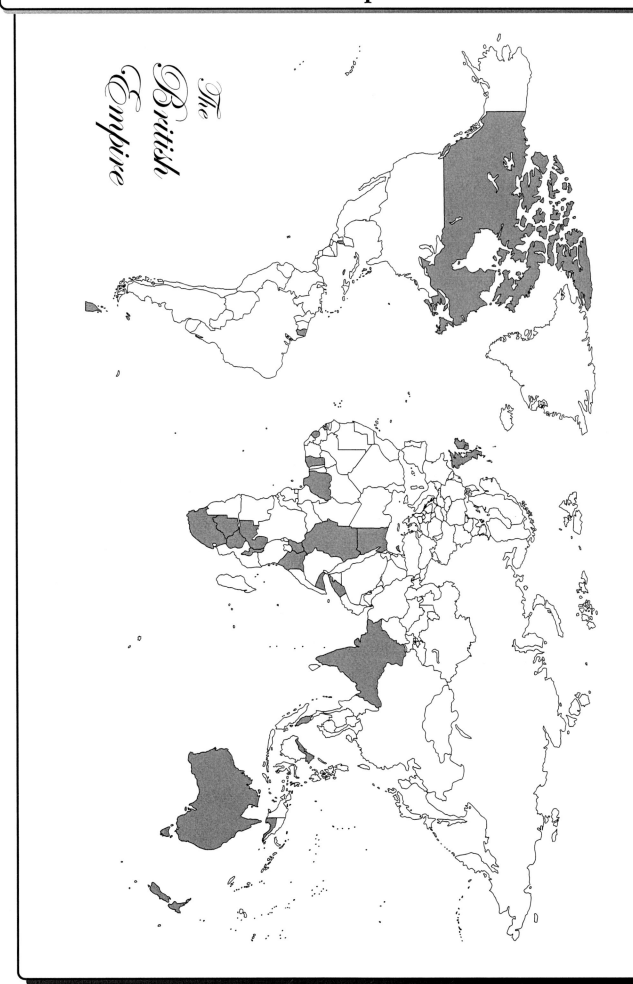

The British Empire

The British Empire in 1900

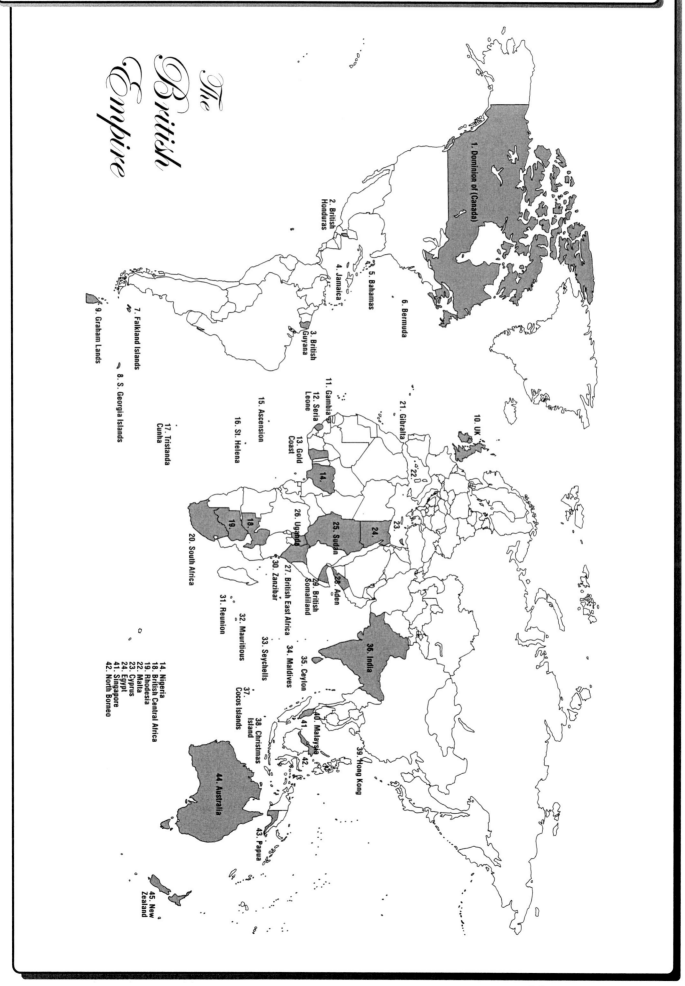

The British Empire

1. Dominion of (Canada)
2. British Honduras
3. British Guyana
4. Jamaica
5. Bahamas
6. Bermuda
7. Falkland Islands
8. S. Georgia Islands
9. Graham Lands
10. UK
11. Gambia
12. Seria Leone
13. Gold Coast
15. Ascension
16. St. Helena
17. Tristan da Cunha
20. South Africa
21. Gibralta
25. Sudan
26. Uganda
27. British East Africa
28. Aden
29. British Somaliland
30. Zanzibar
31. Reunion
32. Mauritious
33. Seychelles
34. Maldives
35. Ceylon
36. India
37. Cocos Islands
38. Christmas Island
39. Hong Kong
40. Malaysia
43. Papua
44. Australia
45. New Zealand

14. Nigeria
18. British Central Africa
19. Rhodesia
22. Malta
23. Cyprus
24. Egypt
41. Singapore
42. North Borneo

The Agricultural Revolution

Objective:

To formulate questions about a picture source.

What you will need:

Copies of Copymaster 25 as an OHT and/or as hard copies for the class.

Teaching point:

The 19th century lends itself to the 'visual starter' approach because of the vast wealth of pictorial material that is available. The aim of such visual starters is to present the class with an intriguing visual source that relates to the main part of the lesson. The source should not be so bizarre that most pupils cannot appreciate it. Pupils are asked to devise questions they want to ask about the picture. Responses show a great deal of differentiation, ranging from simple comprehension questions to very searching high level questions. Some pupils will give 'learned reliability responses', such as 'Is this picture typical?' 'Is it supported by other evidence?' Encourage pupils to focus on the picture, rather than sources in general.

Key words: selective breeding

Activity:

In this book I have included two examples that have worked effectively for me, starters 25 and 27. You will be able to select and collect other visual sources that will appeal to your own classes. An alternative approach is to ask the pupils to annotate the pictures with observations as well as questions.

This starter is more effective if the pupils already have an outline of the Agricultural Revolution.

Ask pairs to make a list of questions they want to ask about the source.

This provides material for a discussion on new farming techniques and selective breeding.

Typical pupil questions:

- Was this a joke of some sort?
- Was the man a midget?
- If it was 1890, why didn't they take a photo?
- Why would anyone want to paint this?
- Is it to show good breeding techniques ~ the prize pig at a farm show?
- Is it exaggerated, or is it a cow with a pig mask?
- Do Yorkshire people always think their stuff is bigger and better? (!)

Challenge: Ask the pupils to find answers to as many of their questions as they can during the lesson.

Links to plenary: In the plenary, ask pupils how many of their original questions they can now answer.

The Yorkshire Hog 1890.

Why was slavery abolished in the British Empire?

Objective:

To rank causal factors in order of importance.

What you will need:

Copymaster 26 cut out into a set for each pair.

Teaching point:

This starter followed a lesson on the factors relating to the abolition of slavery in the British Empire in 1833. Pupils need to have some knowledge of the factors described. Understandably, some teachers are wary of ranking exercises relating to causation, because events are rarely explained by a simple set of rigidly hierarchical causes. However, the aim of this and other such tasks is not to reach a correct answer, but to stimulate thought and discussion. Many pupils find this type of task a high-challenge activity, because they do not have to eliminate any 'wrong' answers. The last card has been included as the only card that can be discounted as untrue.

Key words: abolition

Activity:

Issue Copymaster 26 as a set of cards.

Ask the pupils to arrange the cards in order of importance. Say there is no single correct answer, it is more important that the pupils think about the work they have done on the end of slavery.

Typical pupil responses:

- b or c,

- b and c together, 'because famous individuals were the well known faces of much larger pressure groups,'

- and / or 'because parliament was unlikely to change its mind if most of the middle and upper classes still opposed abolition,'

- and / or 'because if you take b and c out it wouldn't have happened at all, a, d and e helped it to happen at that time, but were of secondary importance.'

- Some say all were linked and put them in a circle, overlapping, except f, which is discounted.

Challenge: Some pupils will find this task difficult, but will be able to select a 'most important cause'.

Links to plenary: N/A

Why was slavery abolished in the British Empire?

a. The West Indies Sugar trade was in a slump, so it made good business sense to end slavery.

b. Christian pressure groups gradually turned public opinion against slavery.

c. Great individuals (such as William Wilberforce and Thomas Clarkson) put pressure on the government.

d. There were several slave rebellions and protests.

e. Britain was rich and could compensate slave owners for freeing their slaves, so that nobody lost out.

f. The British no longer believed that black people were inferior.

19th century attitudes to women

Objective:

To formulate questions about a picture source.

What you will need:

Copies of Copymasters
27a-b as an OHT
and/or as hard copies
for the class.

Teaching point:

The 19th century lends itself to the 'visual starter' approach
because of the vast wealth of pictorial material that is available.
The aim of such visual starters is to present the class with an
intriguing visual source that relates to the main part of the lesson.
The source should not be so bizarre that most pupils cannot
appreciate it. Pupils are asked to devise questions they want to
ask about the picture. Responses show a great deal of
differentiation, ranging from simple comprehension questions to
very searching high level questions. Some pupils will give
'learned reliability responses', such as 'Is this picture typical?' 'Is it
supported by other evidence?' Encourage pupils to focus on the
picture, rather than sources in general.

Key words: handkerchief ~ many pupils have difficulty with this word!
chauvinist ~ a word not directly linked to the source, but often arises from discussion

Activity:

Issue Copymasters 27a-b. Tell the class they show a man's handkerchief sold in 1881, imagining
how the role of women might change by 1981, 100 years in the future.

Ask pairs to make a list of questions they want to ask about the source.

This provides material for a discussion on the role of women in the 19th century.

Typical pupil questions:

- What does the artist want you to think about women?
- This makes fun of women. Is it serious?
- Was this a typical male attitude in 1881, or was the artist a crank?
- How many of the predictions have come true? (Almost all of them, except women who
  join the navy do not go to sea and women in the army are not used as front line combat
  troops.)
- What does this suggest people thought about the roles of women and men?
- Why did people think it was so funny to have women in the navy or police?
- When did women start to take on the roles in the picture? Why?

Challenge: Ask the pupils to find answers to as many of their questions as they can during
the lesson.

Links to plenary: In the plenary, ask pupils how many of their original questions they
can now answer.

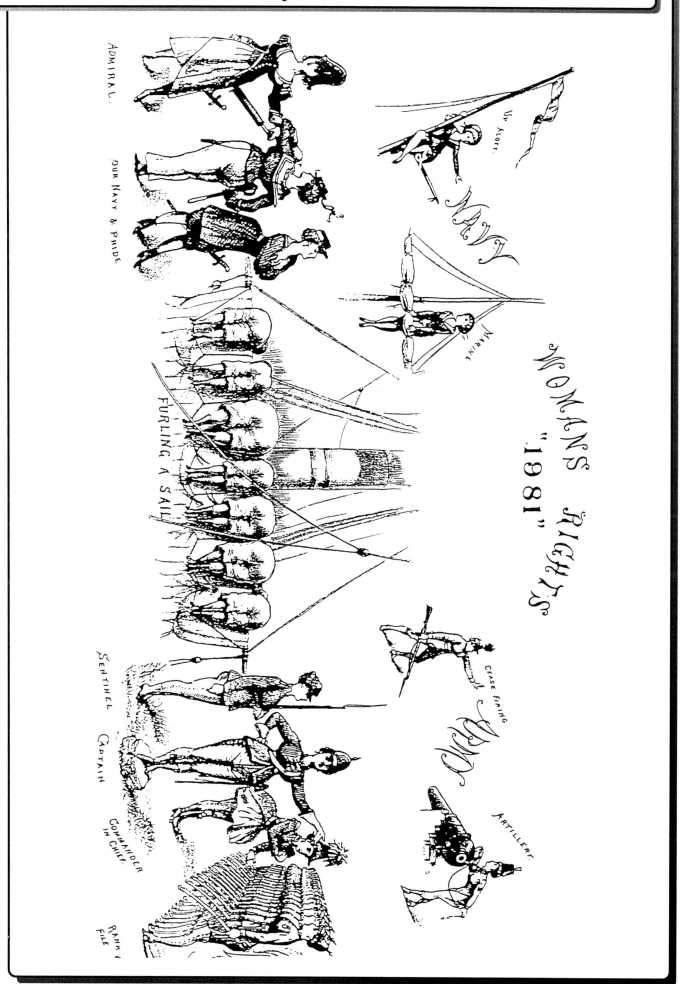

19th century attitudes to women

Factory conditions

Objective:

To use knowledge and understanding of early 19th century factories to classify a set of cards.

What you will need:

Copymasters 28a-b cut out into a set for each pair.

Teaching point:

Early factory conditions and child labour are popular subjects. This starter reviews pupils' understanding of previous work on bad conditions and Robert Owen's factories. Classification can be a very high level activity suitable for the main part of the lesson. In this short starter task, the categories are provided and text is kept to a minimum so that pupils can succeed quickly.

Key words: Review task ~ no new words introduced.

Activity:

Issue Copymasters 28a-b as a set of cards for each pair.

Explain that the cards represent conditions either in a very bad factory or in Robert Owen's factories at New Lanark.

Ask pupils to divide the cards into two categories, a typical 'Dark Satanic Mill' and Robert Owen's mill at New Lanark. If a card applies to both mills, it can be placed in the middle, or in a new category.

(The cards marked • apply to both mills. Although Owen was a humane employer, he could not prevent the noise and dust created by the machinery. Similarly, the need for safety guards was not appreciated.)

Challenge: To write one line captions for the cards, in preparation for a class discussion.

Links to plenary: It is obvious that conditions at New Lanark were much better than elsewhere. Owen made large profits. Ask pupils why so few mill owners followed Owen's example.

A. Machines with no safety guards.

B. Child workers bullied by overseers.

C.

FINES	FINE
Leading window open	1/-
Whistling	1/-
5 minutes late	1/-
Talking	4d

D. Factory school.

E. No pauper apprentices, no child workers under 10 years old.

F. Workers properly dressed, not in rags.

G. Factory doctor.

H. Deafening noise, dust.

I. Limited working hours ~ workers going home in daylight.

J. Pauper apprentices dressed in rags.

K. Decent houses near the factory.

L. Good value factory shops.

M. Institute for adult leisure and education.

N. Child falling asleep from 12+ hour day.

O. Expensive shop which only accepts factory tokens.

Attitudes to native peoples in the British Empire

Objective:

To highlight examples of racism in a 19th century text.

Teaching point:

This starter is useful for a lesson on British attitudes to the peoples of their empire. The extract from *Far Off*, a children's book published by Hatchards of Piccadilly in 1872. The book lists 17 other children's books by the same author. Many pupils are surprised by the extremely racist and patronising tone, and wonder if it is typical of British attitudes. I first used the extract following a lesson on the abolition of slavery. One girl remarked 'I'm sure Wilberforce didn't write this!' This extract can be contrasted with the positive attitudes reflected in some aspects of imperial rule. Some of the sentences have been slightly modernised.

What you will need:

Copies of Copymaster 29a, highlighter pens are useful, Copymaster 29b Teacher page ~ typical pupil responses.

Key words: implicit, explicit, bias

Activity:

Issue Copymaster 29a. Stress that the extract is from *Far Off: or Australia, Africa and America described*, a children's book published in London in 1872.

Ask the pupils to underline any sentences or parts of sentences that suggest that the Australian aborigines are inferior to white people.

Discuss pupil responses.

Challenge: Ask the pupils to identify explicit and implicit criticisms of the natives. Ask the pupils to make a short list of questions they want to ask about the extract. Typical responses: Was this tribe typical? Could the writer speak the native language? Did most British people share such attitudes to native peoples? How long had the writer spent with the natives?

Links to plenary: Having examined British attitudes to their native subjects in more detail, ask pupils if they now consider the extract to be typical.

The Natives of Australia

From *FAR OFF*, a children's book about distant lands, published in London in 1872.

The savages of Australia have neither god nor king, delighting only in eating and drinking, hunting and dancing.

Most men learn to build some kind of houses; but these savages are satisfied with putting a few boughs together, as a shelter from the storm. They do not wish to build better huts, as they are always running about from place to place so that they may get food.

The name for a *wife* or *woman* is 'gin'. Women are the most ill treated creatures in the world. The men beat them on the heads whenever they please, and cover them with bruises. The miserable gins are not beaten only; they are half-starved, for their husbands will give them no food. I have already told you the natives have no GOD; but they have a DEVIL, whom they call Yakoo, or debbil-debbil. When anyone dies, they say 'Yakoo took him.' How different from those happy Christians, who can say of their dead, 'God took them.'

People who do not know God, but only the devil, must be very wicked. They kill many of their babes, that they may not have the trouble of nursing them. Old people they also kill, and laugh at the idea. The bodies of dear friends are treated with honour; they are placed on a high platform for some weeks and then buried. Mothers prize highly the dead bodies of their children. One woman was found carrying the dead body of her ten-year old child on her back for three weeks. She thought she showed her love by keeping it near her for so long a time.

Generally speaking, it is only their *enemies* they eat, and they *do* eat them whenever they can kill them.

It may surprise you to hear that these wild creatures have a turn for music and drawing. Figures showing beasts, fishes and men have been found upon the rocks, and are much better done than could have been supposed.

The Natives of Australia

From *FAR OFF*, a children's book about distant lands, published in London in 1872.

The <u>savages</u> of Australia have <u>neither god nor king, delighting only in eating and drinking, hunting and dancing.</u> *Implies that it is bad not to have a god or king, and that there is more to life than food and dancing.*

<u>Most men learn to build some kind of houses; but these savages are satisfied with putting a few boughs together,</u> as a shelter from the storm. *Implies they are satisfied with a standard below that of most other people, even though they are nomads who do not need a permanent home.* They do not wish to build better huts, as they are always running about from place to place so that they may get food.

The name for a *wife* or *woman* is 'gin.' <u>The women are the most ill treated creatures in the world. The men beat them on the heads whenever they please, and cover them with bruises. The miserable gins are not beaten only; they are half-starved, for their husbands will give them no food.</u> *Explicitly states that women are treated cruelly.* I have already told you the natives have no GOD; but they have a DEVIL, whom they call Yakoo, or debbil-debbil. When anyone dies, they say 'Yakoo took him.' <u>How different from those happy Christians, who can say of their dead, 'God took them.'</u> *The Christian religion is superior.*

People who do not know God, but only the devil, must be very wicked. *Explicit* They kill many of their babes, that they may not have the trouble of nursing them. Old people they also kill, and laugh at the idea. The bodies of dear friends are treated with honour; they are placed on a high platform for some weeks and then buried. Mothers prize highly the dead bodies of their children. One woman was found carrying the dead body of her ten-year old child on her back for three weeks. She thought she showed her love by keeping it near her for so long a time. *Implies that this does not show love, just ignorance.*

<u>Generally speaking, it is only their *enemies* they eat, and they *do* eat them whenever they can kill them.</u> *Explicit ~ cannibals.*

<u>It may surprise you to hear</u> that these wild creatures have a turn for music and drawing. Figures showing beasts, fishes and men have been found upon the rocks, and <u>are much better done than could have been supposed.</u> *Grudgingly admits they are good artists and singers, despite being savages in other respects.*

People and their achievements

Objective:

To match notable individuals and their achievements.

What you will need:

Copymasters 30a-b cut out in a set for each pair (alternative a). One set of Copymasters 30a-b cards (alternative c). Answers on Copymaster 30c.

Teaching point:

Many pupils notice the lack of women in this activity, which represents the lack of opportunities for women in the 18th and 19th centuries. (I decided not to include Florence Nightingale as a 'token' woman!) This could be discussed with the class.

Key words: Revision exercise ~ no new words introduced.

Activity:

Alternative a.

Issue Copymasters 30a-b as a set of cards. The 'name and fame' cards can be two different colours for easier identification.

Ask pairs to match each person with the correct achievements.

Alternative b.

Kinaesthetic. Pupils are given a single card which they copy onto a Post-it note and stick on their forehead. Pupils circulate around the room until they form a pair, and then sit down. This is more time-consuming but many pupils find it more fun to do.

Challenge: Issue only a set of the name cards to each pair of pupils. Pupils write their own 'fame' captions on the blank reverse side.

Links to plenary: Pupils could write additional 'Name and Fame' cards, or 'Place and Fame' cards.

People and their achievements

I.K. Brunel	Richard Arkwright
William Wilberforce	George Stephenson
Lord Shaftesbury	Robert Bakewell
Abraham Darby	Josiah Wedgewood
John MacAdam	Humphrey Davey

People and their achievements

Agricultural pioneer, selectively bred animals.	Ironmaster at Coalbrookedale.
Owned pottery factories and sponsored canal building.	Engineer, designed bridges, ships.
Invented the water frame, making large textile factories possible.	Campaigned for the abolition of slavery.
Railway locomotive designer, mining engineer.	Road designer and builder.
Scientist who invented a lamp for coal miners.	Campaigned for better working conditions and hours, especially for children.

People and their achievements

Answers:

Robert Bakewell	Agricultural pioneer, selectively bred animals.
Abraham Darby	Ironmaster at Coalbrookedale.
Josiah Wedgewood	Owned pottery factories and sponsored canal building.
I.K. Brunel	Engineer, designed bridges, ships.
Richard Arkwright	Invented the water frame, making large textile factories possible.
William Wilberforce	Campaigned for the abolition of slavery.
George Stephenson	Railway locomotive designer, mining engineer.
John MacAdam	Road designer and builder.
Humphrey Davey	Scientist who invented a lamp for coal miners.
Lord Shaftesbury	Campaigned for better working conditions and hours, especially for children.

Badger Publishing Limited
26 Wedgwood Way, Pin Green Industrial Estate,
Stevenage, Hertfordshire SG1 4QF
Telephone: 01438 356907
Fax: 01438 747015
www.badger-publishing.co.uk
enquiries@badger-publishing.co.uk

Badger Key Stage 3 History Starters ~ Book 2

ISBN 1 84424 136 X

Text and original artwork © Phil Suggitt 2003
Complete work © Badger Publishing Limited 2003

Publisher: David Jamieson
Editor: Paul Martin
Designer: Adam Wilmott
Illustrated by Phil Suggitt

Printed in the UK.

Badger Starters

For the Key Stage 3 Core Subjects

Badger Maths Starters by Brian Fillis, KS3 Maths Consultant
"Extremely helpful ~ we are recommending them" *KS3 Maths Consultant*

Year 7	ISBN 1 85880 906 1
Year 8	ISBN 1 85880 907 X
Year 9	ISBN 1 85880 908 8

Badger Literacy Starters by Pie Corbett & Sue Dymoke
"Excellent ~ really, really good" *KS3 Literacy Consultant*

Year 7 Word Level	ISBN 1 85880 860 X
Year 7 Sentence Level	ISBN 1 85880 863 4
Year 8 Word Level	ISBN 1 85880 861 8
Year 8 Sentence Level	ISBN 1 85880 864 2
Year 9 Word Level	ISBN 1 85880 862 6
Year 9 Sentence Level	ISBN 1 85880 866 9

Badger Science Starters by John Parker
"I am really impressed and so are a lot of my schools" *KS3 Science Consultant*

Year 7	ISBN 1 85880 353 5
Year 8	ISBN 1 85880 354 3
Year 9	ISBN 1 85880 355 1

For the Key Stage 3 Foundation Subjects

Badger History Starters by Phil Suggitt

Book 1 (with a Y7 focus)	ISBN 1 84424 135 1
Book 2 (with a Y8 focus)	ISBN 1 84424 136 X
Book 3 (with a Y9 focus)	ISBN 1 84424 137 8

Badger Geography Starters
Fred Martin, Lisa Mitchell, Charlotte Togni and Gary Dawson

Book 1 (with a Y7 focus)	ISBN 1 84424 138 6
Book 2 (with a Y8 focus)	ISBN 1 84424 139 4
Book 3 (with a Y9 focus)	ISBN 1 84424 140 8

Badger Religious Education Starters
Helen Morrison, Jo Weir, Karen Saywood & Simone Whitehouse

Teacher Book with Copymasters	ISBN 1 84424 141 6